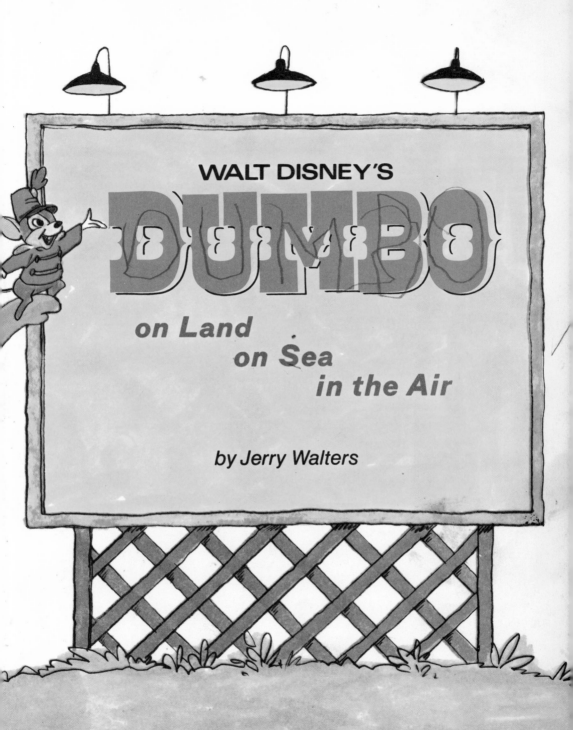

WALT DISNEY'S

DUMBO

on Land
on Sea
in the Air

by Jerry Walters

Random House New York

Library of Congress Cataloging in Publication Data

Walters, Jerry.

Dumbo on land, on sea, in the air.

When the train breaks down on the way to their opening performance, Dumbo and the other circus animals must find other means of transportation.

[1. Circus stories] I. Title. PZ10.3.W203Du [E] 72-7397
ISBN 0-394-82518-7 ISBN 0-394-92518-1 (lib. bdg.)

Manufactured in the United States of America

26112

Mrs. Jumbo put her big, yellow case onto the train.
"That is that!" she said. "Now the circus is ready to go."

All the animals were in their seats.
But the train did not start.
They waited and waited and waited.
The train still did not move.

Finally Mrs. Jumbo
looked out the window.

"Dumbo," she said to her son.
"Go see why the train does not start.
We will be late."

Dumbo went to the front of the train.
There he saw Casey, Jr., the engine.
Poor Casey! He had lost two wheels.
And he seemed to be falling apart.

Dumbo told his mother the bad news.
"Oh, dear," she said. "What will we do?
The circus opens in Boston in just four days."

"I will find a way for us to get there," said Dumbo.
He flapped his long, floppy ears. He flew into the air.
Dumbo was the only flying elephant in the world.
His friend Timothy, the mouse, sat on Dumbo's nose.

Together, Dumbo and Timothy
flew over the city.

"Look!" called Timothy. "A ship.
We can go to Boston on a ship.
It must be fun to travel on the water."

Dumbo landed on the deck
of the great big ship.

"Can you take our circus
to Boston?" he asked
the ship's captain.

"I will be glad to take you,"
said the captain.

Mrs. Jumbo was very happy when she heard the news.

"Follow me," she called to the other animals.

"I will lead you to the ship."

Each animal had his own way
of getting onto the ship.

Mrs. Jumbo walked across a little bridge.
She was so fat that it almost broke in two.

The giraffe grabbed the rail with his long legs.
The bear swung over on a big hook.
The rhino tried to climb through the life-saver.

Look out, everybody! Here comes Tiger Jim on a rope!
If he isn't careful, a flying fox will hit him.

"Glad to see you!" said the captain.
"Please feel right at home here."

The monkeys felt right at home.
They started swinging from the lights.

Mrs. Jumbo went to her room.

"Oh, my," she said. "That bed
looks a little small for me.
I had better see if it fits."
And up the ladder she went.

Crash! Mrs. Jumbo landed on the floor.
The bed was certainly too small.

Harry Hippo wanted to go upstairs.
The stairs were tiny. He was big.
His friends had to push and push
. . . and push.

Wham! They pushed a little too hard.
Harry crashed through the door
and banged into the poor captain.
The captain fell through the steering wheel
and hit the table.

The captain was very, very angry.
"Pack your bags!" he shouted.

"I will not take this circus
any farther. Get off my ship!"

Dumbo and Timothy flew away
from the ship as fast as they could.
Now they had to find another way
to get to Boston.

They did not have much time.
The circus had to be there
in just three days.

Soon they came to an airport.

"Look at that big helicopter," shouted Timothy. "Maybe we can use that. Then *everybody* can fly—just like you and me."

The helicopter man was glad
to follow Dumbo and Timothy
to the ship.

When the animals saw
the helicopter coming,
they all began to cheer.
"Hurray for Dumbo!"
they shouted.

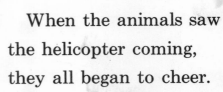

Dumbo's friends began to climb
aboard the helicopter. What fun!
The monkeys ran up the giraffe's neck,
while a big net carried Mrs. Jumbo.
The fox had a nice ride on her trunk.

At last the animals were all set.
Everybody had his own place.
The seal even had water to splash in.
What a good way to travel!

As they rode, they looked out the windows
at the bright blue sky.
They had never gone so fast before.
Flying was certainly fun. . . . But suddenly——

The wind began to blow. The sky grew black.
Lightning flashed and the rain poured down.
The helicopter began to shake.
All of the animals were afraid.

"Dumbo, you must get us out of here!"
shouted Mrs. Jumbo.

Dumbo and Timothy flew down
toward the ground.
It was hard to see in the rain.
But they found a big parking place.
There were trucks and cars on it.
There was also room for a helicopter.

The helicopter landed,
and the animals staggered out.
They felt sick.
But they had to get to Boston.

The bear jumped onto a motorcycle.
The rhino climbed into a car
that was a little too small for him.
Dumbo told the man at the parking lot
that the circus would pay
for the cars and trucks.

Mrs. Jumbo rode in a big truck.
The tiger, the fox and the parrot
rode on top of her.
They had a very good driver.

Harry Hippo had his own little car. It went very fast.
The kangaroo found a wonderful new way to hop—
much faster than the old way!

At last the animals reached Boston.
Dumbo got them there just in time!

"Hooray," shouted the ringmaster.
"Let's get this circus started!"

"Boys and girls! The circus is about to begin,"
called the ringmaster. And begin it did.
Rhino and fox were swinging on their trapezes.
And so were the monkeys.

Mrs. Jumbo rolled around the ring on her ball.

Harry Hippo stood on his head.

Everybody was doing something.

It was truly the best circus anybody had ever seen.

When the circus was over, Mrs. Jumbo hugged Dumbo.
"Son," she said. "I am very proud of you.
Because of your help, the circus opened on time."

Then she added, "And you helped, too, Timothy."
Both Dumbo and Timothy were very, very happy.

THE AGAMENTICUS POEMS:

Voices from York, Maine

Donald Junkins

*Thine age shall be clearer than the noonday;
thou shalt shine forth, thou shalt be as the
morning.*

Job 11:17

Hollow Spring Press

The poems "Trafton Swain, a Barn Sale on Pudding Lane, York, Maine" and "A Hunter Leads Two Brothers to an Abandoned Cemetary" appeared previously in *The Hollow Spring Review of Poetry*, Volume III, Number Two.

Publication of *The Agamenticus Poems: Voices from York, Maine* is made possible by a generous contribution from Rising Paper of Housatonic, Massachusetts. *The Agamenticus Poems* was printed at Quality Printing Co., Inc. of Pittsfield, Massachusetts in cooperation with Hollow Spring Press.

Cover drawing by Fred Becker.

Susan Kelly of Darien, Connecticut, co-proprietor of *A Gravey Business,* provided the inside art of the tree of life, which is an original stone rubbing from a New England cemetery in the seventeenth century.

Publisher and editor of Hollow Spring Press: Alexander Harvey.
Business Manager of Hollow Spring Guild: Paula Harvey.
Hollow Spring Press is a non-profit literary publishing house incorporated and operated by the Hollow Spring Artists and Writers Guild, Inc.

ISBN: 0-936198-10-9

For Daniel,

who ran with me
in the other land.

CHRONOLOGY

Agamenticus, Maine was re-named York in the seventeenth century when Maine lost its provincial status and became part of the Massachusetts Bay Colony. Three gentle-sloping elevations, barely two hundred feet above sea level, still retain the Indian name ("the other side of the river") and comprise the "mountain" near the York River.

Joseph Moody, 1700-1753, served as town clerk, register of deeds, judge, schoolmaster, associate pastor to Samuel Moody at the First Parish church, and ordained pastor of the Second Parish Baptist Church in York. In the fall of 1738 he ascended the pulpit with a white handkerchief draped from his forehead, and wore the veil for the next several years. He was ousted from his pulpit in April, 1739 having been judged "incapable" by a vote of his congregation. Several years after removing the veil he was called back to serve as pastor (Nov. 1749). Moody kept a diary in coded Latin for the four years previous to his marriage to Lucy White of Gloucester in 1724. The diary, which notes an anguished romance with his cousin Mary Hirst while engaged to Lucy, was discovered in 1972 by Raymond Wilbur in the Maine Historical Society in Portland, and translated and published in 1981 by Philip McIntire Woodwell. Moody was the model for the invented character of Father Hooper in Nathaniel Hawthorne's "The Minister's Black Veil."

Olive Williams Junkins left Dover, New Hampshire in 1823 for York, Maine where she "took up residence" with Samuel Junkins, a farmer recently converted to the Cochranite religious sect. Junkins was urging his Baptist brethren to adopt the tenets of Jacob Cochran who was imprisoned at Charlestown in 1819 for "gross lewdness, lascivious behavior and adultery." Olive and Samuel were united in Cochranite fashion (pledging vows and announcing their marriage in the company of other followers), and worshipped in the Baptist Meeting-House in York. Olive was 34 years old, and Samuel, whose first wife's death the year before had left him with their seven children, was 54. Resentment against their Cochranite marriage forced them to legally marry on January 27, 1824—three months after they had been fined and jailed for "willfully disturbing a meeting at the Baptist Meeting-House in York on the Lord's Day."

Townspeople called her Olive Doe the stragling [sic] woman, presumably as a sign of their accusations that she had merely straggled into town and into Junkins' bed. Where she had met him first is not known, nor how she arranged to come to York in 1823. She privately published a partly evangelical, partly historical account of their arrest and imprisonment in the Alfred jail.

The lines: "in league with the stones of the field," "taste in the white of an egg," and "the foolish among you take root" are from the King James version of the Book of Job.

CONTENTS

I.

II.

III.

I.
Personae

Joseph Moody
Samuel Moody
Mary Hirst
Lucy White
Hazel Combs
Sylvester Junkins
Sarah Keen
Samuel Sewall
Flora the Negro
Ebenezer Preble
Humility Preble
Barsham Allen
Trafton Swain
Emaline Quinby
Widow Cutt
Philip Downe
Widow Tomsen
Noah Peck
Abram Nowell
Mrs. Matchet
Joseph Plaisted
Rev. Cooper
The Infant Cooper
Pool
Nutt the Pirate
The Condemned Negro
Neb McIntire

Joseph Moody, schoolmaster in York, Maine
in my 21st year, associate pastor to my father Samuel,
living at home,
January 1722

and I am dark adrift in a skiff
in the white hour of fog, curling
on the lip of a wave my open mouth
cries sounding deaf in this gale
for small crafts, this hour of lips under
the white mouth,
                    for my cousin Mary Hirst
in her chamber, that peapod: frothspeck
under the yearning of my mouth
and I stare the white cloth of the storm
my hand advances on my member, oh Christ
pilot me in my despising of death,
                                    my
father grows white day by day, dear
mother fumbles away from the lucid
light, this white flapsail,
I pollute myself, *Jesu*, the white forearm
of Hirst across my mouth, across

the hall of my father's house, the hovering
of hands, sheet-tearing I fail, I fail,
I hate thee Hirst, I hate thee Lucy White in Gloucester,
you will wear the white veil, and so will I
for Jesus will smite me, Lucy White, Lucy White.

Joseph Moody, My Diary
May 16, 1723 "Very warm. Some air and flying clouds."

I take great delight in my birds,
of which two today are dead,
their beaks exceedingly vivid

and reddish. I hold both
some minutes, prying
their eyes, nubbling

their necks until soiled. Now the sand
shapes them in a single mold
near our fishermen weighing off

their fish. I dally
with the spade, deliberate on
Rev. White's letter, walk

on stilts in the sand. In the family
of late, I am moved
by nothing. Scarcely do I speak

to the point. Cousin Hirst is far
gone, though she yet sleeps
in father's house. Judge Sewall's

verses sting in this. I
am resigned, though I force
the end. Mary Hirst is gone.

Hazel Combs, the potter, seen from a passing wagon.
September 1809

It's a house of black bowl jugs,
hatted pears, and goblets black
as pearl. She digs gray harbor clay
near Kingsbury's landing. Windowsills
of shiny blackberry urns. Hauls
sawdust from Bragdon's mill. Darned
if she didn't line a barrel with little beach
rocks just so. There she sits burling
that charcoal in, fingerworking
the clay. She'll light that barrel and the sawdust
will burn two days.

Hazel lifts those bowls out like busted
clams. The ones that make it
shine right there in her window.

Conversation from the Moody farm across from the site of the Junkins garrison house
April 1980

We've watched those gravestones sliding
toward the Scotland road for years.
One owner hauled the granite posts
for his garden. The new ones
brought a lawyer to keep the young ones
from fixing up the graveyard. Said
it was their land now. The law's
clear, but they all showed up
in a rainstorm and talked it over,
except the woman. She stood
by the car and yelled: *your ancestors*

were prisoners. No one ever done
nothing about it.

Trafton Swain: A barn sale on Pudding Lane,
York, Maine
June 1979

(a woman's voice can be heard next door, singing
a Protestant hymn)

Graveyards, you say. You two fellows
know the graveyard with just one stone in the woods
near Kingsbury Marsh? It's the name
you're looking for, all right. I came across it
hunting. The stone's slanted almost over
but you can read it if you kneel down. Part
of a stone wall goes three quarters
around. One time it must have been a field
but it's all grown up in there now. I
don't know anybody else knows of it but my son
Marvin.

> *. . . just like Jesus to keep me*
> *day by day—*

One fall we tried to straighten it
but it's fast in the ground. I forget the first
name but the last name's same as yours.
The marble back's all brown. The underside's
clear enough where the writing's faced the dirt.
The dates are in the eighteen hundreds.

> *. . . Jesus, Jesus all along—*

I know one other place where there's one stone
marker in the middle of the woods. A little girl's
buried there. The date's 1819. I can't tell
if anyone else's in there with her, nothing
shows for it if they are. She has a last
name I never heard before: Quinby, with an "n."
Emaline Quinby, eighteen months old, born
in Mobile, died here in York. The stone's
just standing in the woods by itself, no
fence, nothing but woods. Just a little
girl. Nice name—Emaline. Emaline
Quinby.

5

Joseph Moody, My Diary
April 1724

On my way to Gloucester I climbed Beacon Hill,
saw seven laden vessels entering the port. I
did not doubt that the Mistress had come. Rev.
Cooper preached to the condemned Negro and I
was much pleased. I saw the unfortunate malefactor
passing through the gates, lifting his head
and his hands toward heaven. Judge Sewall
always receives me kindly. I went astray
on the road from Ipswich through the hills.
At Northend's the woman thought I was
father. At sunset I crossed the ferry
and stayed up late with my love not without
pleasure. I indulged my desire too freely
and at night the semen flowed abundantly.
I spent the morning with Mrs. Matchet
who admonished me not to abandon the preaching
of the gospel. Noah Peck died. At night
I played checkers with my love. Several
vessels taken lately by Nutt the pirate.
The next day I greeted father returning
from the funeral of the infant Riggs. I
sat up three nights with my love until twelve-
thirty and talked in a religious vein, free
from my usual lust, that is, after voluntary
self-pollution. I told my love that I shot
Ebenezer Preble dead when I was eight. I
could not mount my horse for he was nowhere
to be caught. When found, I enjoyed the company
of one Pool for seven miles. I
did not give a cripple anything in Greenland
because I suspected he was not honest. I
made my way from Portsmouth to York
with Joseph Plaisted, through the rain.
At home I was fed fish.

I am Joseph Moody of the Second Parish Church, York,
Maine. At the age of 38 years, I ascend my pulpit
with a white handkerchief draped from my forehead. In
the afternoon, I walk to Berwick, thinking on my
boyhood journal.
October 1738

Consider the gathering of clouds,
the shucking of corn, the relief of husks
and bushels piled. My journal.

The kernal rests
in the quill's black point. I coded it
in Latin until the day I married Lucy
White. Now I wander in my thoughts.
Consider my quill, for I drank much milk
punch, and the Widow Tomsen complained
about her dreaming.

                  January 16, 1723:
I questioned our Negro Flora
on the customs of her nation where certain
old men are able to bring dark matters
into the light, covering their faces
with a disc bound by a leather thong
above. They walk about repeatedly plunging
their hands in water, clapping
with their palms. At length, the bond
being loosed, they make clear

the secret matters. That day I received
material suitable for making shoes.
Neb. McIntire laughed at my uncle
during the prayer. After school he asked me
again and again for permission to go
out. When I was obliged to leave
he wet himself.

Six days earlier I struck Abram Nowell
to the effusion of blood from his nose.

Humility Preble reads on a dune overlooking
York Beach
July 1739

Vases of black raspberry lobes
on a long sleeve of briars
by the white surf. A woman
waits in the unending turning of pages,
her white cotton blouse unbuttoned

at the wrists, the blue veins
chanting her perfectly thin arms.

Barsham Allen's heffers graze in the field next
to the Second Parish Church
August 1741

Under the brown and yellow horse chestnut
trees, the coastal heffers
lounge, unredeemed thighs
spreading the late summer
grass, and the white post office
shades in the sun. The Baptist

church crosses the street,
lurching in the unforgiving light.

A hunter leads two brothers to an abandoned cemetary
with one gravestone: the woods above Kingsbury Marsh,
York, Maine
June 1979

The one who wrote this family book's wrong.
Sylvester's been here a hundred-thirty
years. The stone says it.

> When you said poke a stick in the shallows
> I never had an idea we'd strike
> a marker. Just your fingers around
> the edges, . . . there, you're raising it up—

All this time she's been here. The marble's
good as new: fell over her grave like a cape. Snug
all these years, just leaves and rain, five
hundred seasons aside her father.

> House must be close by. They call that
> foundation-hole beyond the trees the Knight
> place, but I'd guess it's the homestead. These
> woods were fields then. Here,—I can't
> budge it. Sylvester's leaned over to stay.

The widow's in between the lines: these two stones
tell more'n the book:—buried him day before Christmas
1846, twenty-seven years. Two weeks later Mary, just
five. That's enough for one woman.

> She up and left. Maiden name was Keen.
> The book says Sarah Keen. Rest of it's gone.

Look here. It says "S.G." instead of "S.J."
His footstone's wrong. Whoever carved it
had something else on his mind—the family never
noticed. Sarah was gone by then, no one left
to bother. That's when the house went over to
the Knights.

The Widow Cutt remembers Ullapool, Scotland
August 1686

This here cottage by the sea begins
comparisons I pray each day will fill
this life, this window view
of rolled hay, the way the hill
slopes to the river tide, the clover
with its heather tint, salt cod
drying on the rack. The church bell

swings on its hempen track.
                    Who can afford
to remember yesterday? Who
can tolerably think on that other world?

Philip Downe, a soldier, vows never to geek [repent]
though he die on the spot. After imprecations and rant,
he dies in the Junkins garrison.
January 1723

There is only *now,* and the mink
slithering over the rockweed is gone
forever. You dumb seed of Seth,
have you counted the stones
in the north field? How long
can a crow wait? I have crawled
at dusk to the edge of the pit
and marveled at the continuous
sliding of the gravel stones. Have
you known a faithful woman's thigh
that didn't edge away in dream?

I am the Reverend Joseph Moody, removed from my pulpit
in York, Maine for being "incapable." I visit the river
at dusk.
April 1739

If we pray Jesus to open our depths,
we pass a foreground shade and the dreams
of deepest sleep. I pass through such a place
nightly, the fog of mercy's hand. Insects hum
in the warm air; Queen Anne's lace softens
the roadside ditches with the palest stems.
The hushed crickets of the fog shall lead
us, and the white moan of the channel buoy
shall lead us home, but where shall we turn,

where shall we turn, for I am as a young man
using stilts to the hilarity of my friends,
and the burden of my father is great
though I love him. And now call the shore-
birds to their rest, for I come among them
in the dusk to out-heron the blue covehen
in the mussel bed, to stomp the tidal sand

in the awkwardness of my youth where the shell-
dishes of the hooded clams gleam,
for I am the heron of the salt marsh
straw, come from prayer in the fields
in the despair of my lust. And the cormorants

gather on the ledge to dry their wings,
and the gulls rant over their island
in the woebegone fog.

II.
Personae

Olive Williams Junkins
Samuel Junkins
Benjamin Colby
George Stacey
David Tiney
Alexander McIntire, Esquire
Captain Savage
The tall lawyer
Dr. Putnam
David Swett
Elder John Boothby
The minister
Mr. Moor
The sheriff
Young Junkins
Charles O. Emerson
Mr. Junkins' daughter
A tall man at court
The judge
Alfred prison landlady

THE STRAGGLING WOMAN POEMS,
A True Verse Narrative of York, Maine, 1823-1825

1.

Olive Williams Junkins: *I sat under his shadow with great delight,
his fruit sweet to my taste*

I arrive Samuel Junkins on a Saturday, towel
my hair on woolen cloths. He abides
his words, the middle child stands, clover
in hand. The Sabbath following is the first
of my going in,

and causes uneasiness. A wind
rackets the broodloft. I arise
and address them, tell them I remember
the Lord when I was fourteen
illuminate my mind, bring me
sight. Now I am an undone
creature; words deliver me
to their eyes. I close
my testimony — Benjamin Colby edges
near, others shake hands,
call me sister with thanks, the good
loving spirit.
        Mr. Junkins rises in his turn
to improve the meeting house. A black
beetle edges the fourth corner
of the pew, a good sign, a comfortable
season. Mr. Junkins holds all, but David
Swett says they will finish
the meeting and shut him out. Swett
dogged us from the first. I
asked his name in the night: Swett?

It turned out they dug a pit
he fell therein. He left
York and never has been there
since.

2.
From my youth I considered a good name
precious ointment

(she reminisces)
I went to Dover and had a child: I,
a stranger. I dreamed a beautiful
room, the floor of ivory. I could not keep
the wild birds from dirtying it, I
was bid look to the upper corner, — there,
the most beautiful fountain!

I had a child, I dreamed
I was bid lift up a little gate —
I cleansed it, I turned round
and found my room perfectly
dry, except a little pool, oozing.

A child,
I dreamed I was walking a journey,
every person passing threw shovels
full of dirt upon me but it rolled off,
I was not the dirtier: I,

a stranger, a child.
The dreams
have been fulfilled.

3.
Concerning women who prayeth and prophesyeth:

The next Sabbath: no minister preaching
at the meeting house. David Tiney
and George Stacey cast looks into my meditation,
came to my pew to carry
me out in silence. Mr. Junkins' son
and daughter said I should not be
carried out — Tiney & Stacey
sat out to press in,
                    young Junkins caught
hold of the pew door. They
said they would come
in if they had to tear the pew
down. Words broke
between them and the lad. They
did not get me out,
and returned disappointed as bears, bereft
of their prey.

4.

A man came, advised us to marry
according to law:

Mr. Junkins and I spoke our piece: we
married agreeably
to the laws of God. The man rattled from his throat
on God: He would not protect
us, the state prison was our portion
and I the means bringing the family
to poverty and crazy too: the only thing
that would clear me.

             Mark!
A few days later the rattler
was arrested passing counterfeit
money, put in jail, condemned at court, six
months solitary

confinement. We're peaceably
at home without being molested
or made afraid. Yesterday
I lifted a rock in the yard: a fair
small creature
lifted his foot at me.

5.
It really appeared to me they had lost my name
in the fog

while I was rejoicing in the white stone
and a new name: I was called Olive
Williams, alias Olive Doe Straggling
Woman. Benjamin Colby caught me by the collar
of my great coat, with violence jerked me
out of the pew, from the pew out the door. We
owned several pews in the Meeting-house.
Is this the land

where we can worship God under our own vine
and fig tree without being molested
or made afraid? My hip
smarted not a little on the way
home. The path turned
a heavy way.

6.
Man's innocence, lost in the garden, must be
restored to recover him:

Esquire McIntire and Captain Savage
came to our house with twenty, desiring
to place us from the reaches
of pretended saints and possums,
purveyors of underbelly heat. We told
them our faith: we took each other
before thirty witnesses—
                              in turns,
Esquire McIntire believed us conscientious:
we should enjoy faith as well
as others: *I pronounce*
you man and wife.
                    Dr. Putnam
said it was a good loving time: the hatchet
ought to be buried.
                    Colby was willing: *I have nothing*
against Junkins or his wife. (The same crowd
of tongues murmuring yesterday
we should be put in the state
prison.) The next day

the tall lawyer said April court
should not pass without our being
indicted. In less
than five weeks, that lawyer
was put under the clods.

7.
Scripture says if anything is revealed to one
that setteth by, let the first hold his peace.

In the Meeting-house
Elder Boothby rendered himself impolite
and went right against the Scripture: he would not hold
still. When the minister closed his sermon, I
told them it was something with me
as with the bush that Moses saw on fire
but not consumed. *I love God,*
every creature he made looks precious,

                    I am willing
to go bound to Alfred prison, there to die.
Elder Boothby broke in again: it was communion
with them, I was a spectator. But
I tell you it was a heavenly time
for me. I could say with the spouse: *if*
you see my beloved, tell
him I am sick, of love . . .

8.
We long to see the King's highway cleared
so that his subjects can run an errand without harm:

What does Mr. Colby think of saying before all
the gentlemen at our house he had nothing
against Junkins or his wife, was willing
to bury all that was past, then go and indict us
before the Grand Jury and swear
we willfully disturbed his meeting? Colby

swore Mr. Junkins put his hand
on the pew and rapped on purpose to disturb
when his hand was not next the banister
but was in his lap and he would change it
from one knee to the other. When it was on the side
next to the wall, his knee made a little noise. I
was going to put out my hand
to move his knee, but remembering one
cursed for attempting to steady the Ark
I dare not do it. Supposing

it was as Colby said: he well
knew Mr. Junkins was hard of hearing, if his hand
made a noise he could not hear it. Besides
Colby knew him for twelve
years: he knew when Mr. Junkins
had anything to do for God, he had a trembling
in his hand and could not help it.

9.
Elder John Boothby said he never knew of a woman
taking the lead, but that people came to nothing.

Elder John, I cite you Judges: the Lord
sells Sisera into the hands
of a woman. By the hand of a woman
a nail is driven through his temple
and he dies. You want witnesses?
I'll give you a cloud from the Old
and the New: Anna the prophetess;

the woman who first preaches the risen
Jesus and runs trembling
with news.
            John Boothby, read
the book of Judith. God delivers
the whole city of Bethulia
into the hands of a woman. Esther
the Queen delivers
the whole nation of the Jews. If

your weakness is exposed
by a woman, you have nothing
to complain of.

10.
Come, gather yourselves together unto the Supper
of the Great God: eat the flesh of Kings, the flesh of Captains,
the flesh of Mighty Men, the flesh of Horses:

On the Sabbath before Thanksgiving, Mr. Colby
and Mr. Moor came to our pew: *the civil*
authority should take care of you for living
with Junkins. They had no fellowship
with him, told me they were agoing
to carry me out. I
told them I came
peaceably in and could when ready
go without help. I

then felt like a full pot. Such
sweet union with God my Father, Jesus
Christ my elder Brother. I was willing
to take life in my hand, go
forth: I arose, told the people —

Next week the sheriff
came and conveyed me to his house.

11.
I told the family, according to my feelings
a sheriff was coming:

Before twelve and one o'clock
the sheriff came with a warrant. I felt
the most exquisite thirst. I fell
and they raised me up. One
of our neighbors carried me about three
quarters of a mile, got
help, took me out of the chaise. Some
standing by said they made as bad
a piece of work as though I had been lead. They
carried me to an armchair in Charles
O. Emerson's office.
              Mr. Junkins' daughter
came much grieved. I asked to sit
on the floor, my head
in her lap. Colby
came by: *You've got an easy*
seat. He looked down
as though I was a criminal for murder.
The Justices who had tried
us before would have nothing to do
about it, — they had to hunt
one.

    I was put under
bond for sixty dollars, cognized
to appear at Alfred next
term. Esquire McIntire
and Captain Savage became bail. Benjamin

Colby since fell down a steep place, —
all his bowels gushed out.

12.
In what they know naturally as brute beasts
they corrupt themselves.

Remember the tall man at court
who stood near the judge muttering
against us? He called me "the woman,"
Mr. Junkins "the man." *The woman*
has been living several months
with the man before marriage
as a bunter. I ask Mr. Tallman
how he knows that? According to the law
of the land he ought to smart
for abusive language.

       Another thing:
he was not married three months
and he became a father.

13.
The Alfred prison — we covered ourselves
in our little couch without supper:

Alexander McIntire came twice
the next afternoon: *you must go*
to York where you have more
friends, though in prison. For supper
we ate crusts of bread, a little
beef, one cracker, a small piece
of mouldy cheese, all
in a tin basin. Mr. McIntire

went to the boarding-
house and brought my trunk: night
clothes, some stores. This
was no small kindness to me. I
was out of health
a far time.
      Mr. Junkins and I committed
ourselves to God, retired to my straw
couch, as easy to us as a bed
of down. We did not awake until the sun
was up.

14.
The Alfred prison: the bed was my pulpit

as soon as the spirit ceased:
I laid myself down.
                    About eight
they came with wood and victuals
as the night before. I said
I should be glad of something
warm and comfortable
if they could — if not, we wished
nothing.
                    In a few minutes
the landlady came in a great passion
demanding what we expected being
prisoners. My husband said we deserved
neither death nor bonds
and since a worse prison than this lay
somewhere else, he advised she show
a little humanity toward fellow
mortals. She said the tea
was hot and good. I
asked her to grant a cup
and saucer. She refused
saying the treatment was good
enough for Cochranites.

                    I left
them some advice: use prisoners
better. I heard
the most pitiful cries
almost perishing with the cold
by reason of no bedclothes. I
heard since, they were lousy.

15.
A word to the judge and jury:

You and I will appear
before the Judge of all
the earth. There the high title
of judge will not gain
His favor nor the mean name
of Cochranite His frown: we
shall be judged according to the deeds
done in the body

whether they be good
or whether they be evil.

16.
Our cities are according to their numbers
a complete sample of Old Jerusalem:

For a sign, some will have to wear girdles,
some to go naked —

                    this moment

while I write, my heart, it swells. If
I lift my hands away from the fatherless, let
my right arm fall from my shoulderblade, my
other arm break from the bone —

One invitation more I give: *leap,*
dance, cast out devils,
rejoice with me in the white stone.

III
Personae

Joseph Moody
Nutt the pirate
The Gatherer
The Other Mouth
The Tongue
A Stranger
Joshua Nowell
Cousin Coffin
Sarah Johnson
Sam Bass
Mr. Banks
Frank Beaver
George Whitefield
John Milberry
Jeremy Dummer

Arthur Bragdon
Hannah Bane
Marvin Swain
Lid Sewall
Dependence Stover
Josiah Moulton's wife
Mary Hirst
Trafton Swain
Jo Bragdon
Lissey Milberry
Cousin Bradbury
Father Samuel Moody
Bragdon's niece
Day's brother

I am Handkerchief Moody of York, Maine
May 1739

asked by The Gatherer to counterattack
miniatures,
              to separate broodtongues
in the rattle-drawer, asked to size
the Other Mouth among our midst,
for the Lord decries henbane at dusk. He
loathes the catnip fit which outlasts
the eclipse.
I preach whitebone and gauntrot,
for I am in league with the stones of the field:

I pray the long prayer of the wrapup
under the white eyes, for The Gatherer
has guided me to Bragdon's house, and my
broodseed is scattered across York.

You want me to talk sense about the veil
when I have a roaring gut, and the boxes
rot in the field? While you skant your noses
and cast lots? Nutt the pirate is a fingerling
on the waters of our ways: there is a well
nearer The Tongue for us all.
Yea, you ask for the long prayer
from the back of the church, and shudder

but The Gatherer blesses the tie
that binds while we are absent One
from the Other in our doom.

31

Hannah Bane writes in her diary after Josha Nowell leaves York
October 1673

Remember our Scotland and the ruins
of Varrich Castle in the rain?
— how you slid down the nibbled grass
greener than paint, and pretended
to leap from the unbecoming cliff?
— how I called to you later

on the Thyrso Road across the wind
and you called nothing has changed?

The Mount Agamenticus gateway: Marvin Swain walks with a stranger in the woods above Kingsbury Marsh June 1979

This road goes up the mountain, though it aint
a mountain, just the highest hill in these
parts. The homesteads've fallen in but for
the root cellars. Burial places
grown up around with trees and brush, — s'shame.
Them people set store by this here land, clearing,
piling walls. Granite's what they could handle, —
cut them root-cellar slabs thick

as this'n over the brook, oxen
done that. See that slab straight up
there? Used to be one opposite. A fellow
come with a pick-up and hauled it out —
leaning almost over,

but he couldn't get this'n. I measured twelve
feet above ground, no telling how deep
it's under. Someone had a mind for it to stay
put. Beats me why anyone'd want either one.
Evidence, you say? I guess probably. It's
a gateway of some sort. Two-three
times a year I come by hunting. I
think of them oldtimers going by taking
no notice, going on to what they was going
on to. They knew they was passing through. Go

ahead and push — try both arms against it,
it won't budge. Imagine that fellow
in the truck, trying to pull it out,
having to give up on it?

I am Handkerchief Moody of York, Maine, under
sentence of confusion. I preach to those who will listen
on the Oyster River Plain, watching
January 1740

The bloodlines piercing the white clouds.
See! the great mouth of mimicking Micah,
the kingfishers prating in the pulpit,
they say moody Moody, I say look
on these baptizing hands that tossed the clods
on Lucy's pine box next to little Lucy's pine
box. Look on these burying eyes, for I escaped

by divine aid a snare set by Satan before my
wedding day. I turned my face away
from cousin Coffin uncovering herself, for desire
worked in my flesh. I buried Dependence
Stover not twenty-four hours old. You say
I am incapable but I have looked for cows
in the morning, I have cautioned Hannah Bane
for laughing in public, I have seen the moon
encircled as if by a ring. I have picked

cherries for Lid Sewall. I have cast lots
and the lot fell on Job 40:4. I have seen
the wife of Josiah Moulton lying with arms bared
to her undergarment after she gave birth
to a dead child. I have taken sage, water,
and vinegar and defiled myself four
consecutive days. I have watched cousin
Bradbury cut a hole for fruits. I
have watched Sarah Johnson wearing a hat
at noon. I have consulted Mr. Banks
about the suicide of Sam Bass. I have felt
the hunter's leaden ball pass
my head, I have dismissed school early

to go strawberrying with cousin Hirst.

Mary Hirst composes verses for meditation at the Young
Christian Improvement Society, disapproved by Father
Samuel Moody
June 1722

Crows tip-toe
the rockweed beach, the late summer
mouth of the cove is dry;

I pray for the openness of this day,
the last pale raspberries on my tongue,
and the single daisy by the road;
the clear remembrance of last night's dream,
the white froth of yesterday's storm's wave,
and the brown-eyed Susan's curtsy
in the wind;

I pray for solitude's white pearl of peace
from the blue mussel's side.

The Homestead
June 1979

We rounded the turn in the road
and saw the cellarhole among the heavy brush: a blue
agate pan with birdshot holes rusting
in the yardweed by a granite doorstep. We
picked up two red bricks caked
with dirt, scuffed through the spirea
for evidence. The graveyard told us what
we came for: we found it later, by accident.

> *Jesus of the weeds leap our stone*
> *hearts, touch our bones . . .*

Townsfolk in York knew the place
but had the name wrong. Trafton Swain
and blind Frank Beaver put us on to it. What
Trafton said about the horse bones got us circling
the clearing: "The old Day
place, — hasn't been anybody there for years.
Somebody finally tore it down and hauled
off the boards — I noticed while hunting last
fall that the field's plowed. They say
Bragdon's niece tried a garden but gave
it up. The ground's good enough after all
these years, but the place is hard to get to,
what with the way the roads are in the spring.
There's a pile of horse bones
out back. They say Day's brother dumped
his dead horses on the pile and left them to per-fume
the woods."

> *Peat moss, white pines hold us*
> *snug: bones be not vain in snow . . .*

I stubbed against a half-buried wheel
beside the pasture road leading to the woods.
Frank Beaver had talked spirits about the place
as if they'd touched his face: a friend
brought him in a jeep to walk the ground he hayed
as a hired hand forty years ago: "To feel
the place like it is now, with the lilac

36

big as a tree spreading over the knocked-in
root cellar, the apple trees brittle
and stumpy, the crunched-in pails turning up
everywhere through the woods, you'd think
the place was dead, the lives of all
those people withered off somewhere.
It aint so. There's spirits about the place
every which way you turn."

Turn through the woods, turn over
the withered days . . .

"Not ghosts? Call them by your own name.
They're near every old bucket
and pan in the woods. Something
hauled off those buckets, not just where the barn
was, but beyond the watering pond, the pastures
further on, now grown up pine. When the softwood
set in, the maples gave out, and other things.
Thick pines kept the sun out, the woods
got that moist smell — makes you feel
something alive was there the moment
before you stopped to listen."

Good Jesus, sleep on our bones,
dust the gone fields . . .

My brother called from the corner
of the field, have I found anything? I call
no, Frank Beaver's voice talking inside
my head: "Three years ago I crawled
into the corner of the root cellar, still half
a room, the granite slab over my head seven
inches thick, four by eight feet, made the same
as a tomb in Egypt, thick as a door on a bank
safe. I wasn't in there a minute before I
had to get out and keep going. Whatever it was
pressing down on that slab pressed down
on me. I felt it sure as I'm standing here. If
you go out to the grown-over graveyard, you'll
see what I mean."

While we were absent one
from the other, we lay in waiting
rooms . . .

I find the horse bones; my brother
comes on the old well and a second road
leading to the back pastures. Walking
to the east field, he yells, "Over
here."
   One of the grave-slabs is lying
in a wheelrut, broken in half, run over
by a hunter's jeep. Two stones upright,
another face-down under four inches of damp
pine needles and peat. We find it,
poking a stick. My brother says, "It's
like they've been waiting all these years."

> *Pans, stones, pass over*
> *my bones . . .*

"Or for anybody that takes an interest. Frank
Beaver says it's spirits that got these crunched-in
buckets strewn all over the woods."

> "More like crazy errands, farmgirls and boys
> daydreaming woods when they had business
> with buckets."

> *Busy with daydreaming: bucket*
> *bucket, who's got the bucket? . . .*

"How'd they get strewn? Why leave a good
bucket out to rot? Even if these woods were fields,
every one is all stove in."

> "Good intentions on a clear day get turned
> around if your thoughts get going lonesome
> and wild. The rusty file we found by that old
> maple? Just the signs of a day spent fixing
> a wagon axle in a field. The buckets are what's left
> of human neglect and human need. The stoving in's
> from hunters."

> *All the pines are grass*
> *blades: hunters*
> *walking; drifted snow . . .*

"The hunters have been here. Only what people
feel about the law protects the burial
grounds in the woods. The law
that couldn't keep them from being disturbed
when alive can't keep them from it when dead."

Wind wrap our bones, wind
keep our woods . . .

"It's the smell of autumn, the feeling
of rain before winter, — *that's* near about."

"That and our coming on the graves by accident,
believing what they told us in town, finding
those markers with our family names, not one
slab with Day or any other name not ours.
— Can't you see them carrying the long
boxes through the field to the woods,
standing in rain and sun, walking back
to the house?"

Walking and standing, lying down:
Jesus of the rain, the close dark
rain . . .

"Something about this place
says spirits all right, but not the kind
that stomp the back stairway at night
to claim your mind: the spirits I'm talking
put things in front of your eyes so's you'll take
notice of what seemed like clutter before, things
that lasted through the years as castoffs: pails
and bottles and twisted pans. The need
they have is like our need to touch a face
with our fingers, the spaces in the air
where flesh and blood passed those times
before. Invisible paths are all around us
here, footsteps we can't see, handprints,
places where they sat down in the middle of the woods
and drank water from a jar."

I am Handkerchief Moody of York, Maine, who sits at the back of the church, a rotting stick
March 1744

and prays the long prayer for visiting
tongues, and Whitefield wipes the spittle
from his mouth at the end, his sermon
said, his crossed-eyes focussing Moody
of the white veil, and I pray
the long prayer of bones and thin

hands, the lead ball creasing the head
of my member, the prayer of stilts
by Jo Bragdon's pond, the petition of white
clouds and the tomb's wall,
the Moody grace at the end, the mouth
of Mary before the white veil, raiment

gleaming before the Magdalen's open mouth,
the scabs under the bandages falling,
don't touch me, DON'T TOUCH ME cross-
eyes, look at me and learn: my Lucy
knows, she shows my dead girlchild Lucy
through the white veil, and I pray
the gathering of my lost horse in Berwick,
the swarm of bees at Dummer's
farm, the increase of rulers
to strike the Latin text. I speak

in the tongue of Old Parish Town, the clean
tongue of distant Skye, the tongue
of the unreconciling grave nearby.

I am Handkerchief Moody of York, Maine, invited
to come again among the people, and preach
November 1749

  The foolish among you take root
and you judge me sound

for the farmhouse calms
while the log burns,

and the youngest child sleeps
as her nightmare stalks,

and the heated glass
changes its color not one shade,

and the polluted well
develops no stench in time,

so I have removed the veil these four years,
and the glaze hardens my eyes

for you hope for taste in the white
of an egg, and I swallow

these thoughts as I stand here
before you. I am Lazarus

not returned from the dead.

John Milberry drowns off the Isle of Shoals. His wife
Lissey sings along at home, after the service
February 1723

Blue mussel blue, my love has sailed
    on the Isle of Shoals
    and the rocks have downed him there
    and the sea has claimed him there

Blue mussel blue, my bed is soft
    in the harbor still
    and my love has found me there
    and my love has claimed me there

Blue mussel blue, the nights are long
    on the Isle of Shoals
    in the harbor still
    in my soft soft bed

And the moon is down, blue mussel blue
    the sails are torn
    the sheets are new
    blue mussel blue, blue mussel blue

Colophon

The Agamenticus Poems has been designed by Alexander Harvey and printed at Quality Printing Company, Inc., of Pittsfield, Massachusetts, in cooperation with Hollow Spring Press of Chester, Massachusetts. The text is Garamond type. The paper is Desert Stone and has been manufactured by Rising Paper of Housatonic, Massachusetts.

This edition consists of one thousand copies, of which fifty have been numbered and signed by the author.